Michelle
OBAMA

Michelle OBAMA

FROM CHICAGO'S SOUTH SIDE
TO THE WHITE HOUSE

Marlene Targ Brill

LERNER PUBLICATIONS COMPANY · MINNEAPOLIS

The images in this book are used with the permission of: © Ethan Miller/Getty Images, p. 2; © Stan Honda/AFP/Getty Images, p. 6; © Paul J. Richards/AFP/Getty Images, p. 9; The White House, p. 11; Hobcaw Barony archive/Transparencies, Inc., p. 12; Courtesy of Frank Martinez, Jr., p. 19; Whitney M. Young Magnet High School, p. 21; AP Photo/Peter Morgan, p. 22; 1988 Harvard Law School Yearbook, Courtesy of Special Collections, Harvard Law School Library, p. 25; © Steve Liss/Time & Life Pictures/Getty Images, p. 27; INS News Agency Ltd./Rex Features USA, p. 30; AP Photo/Frank Polich, File, p. 33; Vandell Cobb/Ebony Collection via AP Images, p. 34; AP Photo/The Plain Dealer, Scott Shaw, p. 36; © Ron Sachs-Pool/Getty Images, p. 38; AP Photo/Pablo Martinez Monsivais, p. 39.

Front Cover: Joyce N. Boghosian/The White House.

Text copyright © 2010 by Marlene Targ Brill

Lerner Publications Company
A division of Lerner Publishing Group, Inc.
241 First Avenue North
Minneapolis, MN 55401 U.S.A.

Website address: www.lernerbooks.com

Library of Congress Cataloging-in-Publication Data

Brill, Marlene Targ.
     Michelle Obama : from Chicago's South Side to the White House / by Marlene Targ Brill.
        p.   cm. — (Gateway biographies)
     Includes bibliographical references and index.
     ISBN 978-0-7613-5033-0 (lib. bdg. : alk. paper)
     1. Obama, Michelle, 1964-–Juvenile literature. 2. Presidents' spouses—United States—Biography—Juvenile literature. 3. Legislators' spouses—United States—Biography—Juvenile literature. 4. African American women lawyers—Illinois—Chicago—Biography—Juvenile literature. 5. Chicago (Ill.)—Biography—Juvenile literature I. Title.
     E909.024B75 2009
     973.932092—dc22 [B]   2009007200

Manufactured in the United States of America
1 2 3 4 5 6 – BP – 15 14 13 12 11 10

CONTENTS

Michelle Obama waves to the crowd before she speaks at the Democratic National Convention in Denver, Colorado, on August 25, 2008.

Craig Robinson stepped forward to talk about his sister, Michelle Robinson Obama. It was August 25, 2008, opening night of the Democratic National Convention. Delegates to the convention would select the Democratic candidate for president. A short video outlined his sister's life as a devoted daughter and sister, successful lawyer and administrator, and loving wife and mother. Craig spoke fondly of his kid sister, who was twenty-one months his junior. He talked about her work on issues affecting women, children, and communities. But none of these stories prepared the audience for hearing from Michelle, the woman who could become the next First Lady.

The convention crowd cheered as Michelle Obama took center stage and hugged her brother. At five feet eleven inches, she towered over the lectern. Thousands of people at the convention shouted and waved blue and white signs with her name on them. Others pumped posters in the air that read "Change We Can Believe In"—a slogan from Barack Obama's presidential campaign.

As keynote speaker, Michelle wanted them to know that her husband would be the best candidate for president. Michelle was known as an inspiring public speaker. Still, campaign managers worried. Usually a private person, Michelle preferred staying out of the limelight. She remained cautious about politics and politicians. Critics had already faulted some of the things she'd said on the campaign trail. This convention was a major event seen by many millions of people nationwide on television and websites. Most of those people had never heard of Michelle Obama. Could she capture the nation's heart at this important time in her husband's campaign?

Michelle began quietly to tell Barack's and her stories. They had both come from modest means. Yet both lived the American dream. With a good education, hard work, and strong beliefs, they had become the first African American couple with a shot at the

"AND IN MY OWN LIFE, in my own small way, I've tried to give back to this country that has given me so much. That's why I left a job at a law firm for a career in public service, working to empower young people to volunteer in their communities. Because I believe each of us...has something to contribute to the life of this nation."
—Michelle Obama, speech at the DNC, 2008

Michelle Obama introduced herself to the country with her speech at the convention in 2008.

White House. As Michelle said, they believed that "you work hard for what you want in life; that your word is your bond . . . ; that you treat people with dignity and respect, . . . even if you don't agree with them."

Michelle encouraged everyone to work together to fulfill all the nation's hopes. She urged listeners to join her in Barack's journey. She asked them to vote for her husband to be the Democratic candidate for president of the United States.

After she stopped talking, the audience broke into wild applause. Michelle took in the moment. The reserved girl from Chicago's South Side had found her public voice, and the audience had listened.

South Side Girl

Michelle liked to tell people that she was simply a South Side girl. Chicago, where she was born and raised, has an unusually strong tradition of neighborhoods. Even people who move away continue to define themselves by the old neighborhood where they played and went to school as youngsters. For Michelle, that neighborhood was South Shore on Chicago's South Side.

When Michelle was growing up, Chicago was a segregated city. African Americans crowded into chunks of the South Side and West Side, and white people from different ethnic groups claimed the other areas. The South Shore neighborhood extended from Lake Michigan westward about three miles. It covered blocks of well-kept single-family homes and apartment buildings.

African Americans started moving into South Shore during the 1960s. Michelle's family—Marian Shields Robinson, Frasier Robinson III, and Craig—probably lived slightly north of South Shore when Michelle LaVaughn Robinson was born on January 17, 1964. Michelle's birth occurred six months after President Lyndon Johnson signed the Civil Rights Act. The law banned discrimination and helped open housing to African Americans. Michelle's parents seized the opportunity to move into a less crowded part of the city. They rented about 1,100 square feet on the second floor of a red brick bungalow owned by Michelle's great-aunt.

Michelle and her brother Craig are just twenty-one months apart in age. Here the Robinson family *(left to right)*, Craig, Frasier, Marian, and Michelle, pose for a photo when Michelle was just a baby.

By the time Michelle's family moved into South Shore, the area contained mostly black working-class families. "The neighborhood felt more like an African American suburb than an urban experience," said South Side college teacher and reporter Stephen Garnett. "We knew we were black but didn't think about it."

Family Roots

To know Michelle, those close to her say, people must understand her parents and their proud but challenging history. Both of Michelle's parents trace ancestors back to slavery days. Her family roots extend throughout the segregated South.

Michelle's great-great-grandfather on her father's side, Jim Robinson, was born in 1850. The tall, hard-working man slaved in mosquito-infested rice fields on the Friendfield plantation in Georgetown, South Carolina. After the Civil War (1861–1865), slaves were

Slaves stand in front of their cabin near Georgetown, South Carolina. Jim Robinson lived nearby on a similar rice plantation.

freed, but Jim stayed on the plantation to get married and farm a small plot of riverfront land. Although he never learned to read, he and his descendants emphasized the value of education and hard work.

As years passed, the Robinsons found ways to get an education. Michelle's grandfather, Frasier Jr. (1912–1996), graduated from high school, which at that time was an amazing accomplishment. Friends knew him as a good student who had a way with words. But hostility toward blacks made it hard for him to find work beyond the local sawmill, even with his education.

Frasier Jr. followed a friend to Chicago in search of a better job. He faced difficulties there too. Frasier Jr. was a skilled carpenter. Carpenters belonged to unions, or organized groups of workers. But unions then would not let in black workers. Without a union card, employers would not hire him. He left his wife, LaVaughn, and their five children in Chicago to hunt for better work elsewhere. Without his income, LaVaughn, Michelle's grandmother, found no other choice but to accept welfare. Their eleven-year-old son, Frasier III, took a job delivering milk to help pay the family bills.

After fourteen years, Michelle's grandfather returned to Chicago. He found a long-term job with the U.S. Post Office, but his pay remained low. He and LaVaughn lived in a cinder-block public housing apartment on Chicago's South Side. "He was proud of his lineage [family line]," Michelle remembers. "But there was a discontent about him."

After Frasier Jr. retired, he and LaVaughn moved back to Georgetown. Michelle's father, Frasier III, remained in Chicago and married Marian Shields. Marian's family came from Mississippi and Kentucky. Before slaves were freed, one of Marian's grandmothers cooked and cleaned for slave owners.

MICHELLE RECALLS visits with her large extended family of Robinson aunts, uncles, and cousins. But they never talked about family history.

The Importance of Family

Michelle's parents upheld the same sense of pride, hard work, and drive as their ancestors, sometimes despite great hardships. Her father worked as a pump operator at Chicago's water filtration plant. In Chicago, city jobs came from political connections. To get a city job, you had to know a politician or a politician's relative or friend. To move up to the foreman job, Frasier volunteered off-hours to hustle votes for the mayor.

The family wasn't rich. In fact, their tiny second-floor home contained only one bedroom. Craig and Michelle shared the small living room that was divided by panels into two even smaller bedrooms and a study space. But Frasier earned enough money so Marian could stay home and raise their children.

When Michelle was a baby, thirty-year-old Frasier learned that he had multiple sclerosis, a disease that causes nerve problems and difficulty with muscle control. Falling, numbness, and stiffness followed, and he eventually walked with two canes. Yet, he never complained about his illness or missed a day of work. Frasier's positive, can-do attitude had a huge impact on his children. "Seeing a parent with a disability moving through the world and living life as if that disability didn't matter always made us think," Michelle said. "What do we have to complain about? . . . We are healthy, we're happy, and our father is struggling to get out of bed."

A close-knit family provided the framework for Michelle and her brother to thrive. Marian and Frasier offered a stable and loving two-parent home. The family ate dinner together every night. The adults encouraged their children to speak out, take chances, and be brave enough to risk making mistakes. Marian often repeated: "Don't let people stop you," and "don't be a follower."

Michelle's mother ran a tight ship at home. She believed that "structure and consistency and chores" held the family together as Frasier's health declined. Marian thought discipline and chores taught her children the importance of being responsible. Each day Michelle and Craig made their beds. They alternated washing dishes every other day. Michelle scrubbed the bathroom on Saturdays, including the floor and toilet. Marian made sure that her children budgeted their allowance and time wisely.

Even though they seemed strict, both parents enjoyed a good time. Marian and Frasier encouraged activities that stretched their children's minds and bodies. Family nights included reading, Scrabble, and sports—activities that continue to be favorites. The Robinsons set aside Saturday nights for board games, such as Chinese checkers, chess, checkers, and Monopoly. Relatives gathered at their home to share meals, listen to jazz music, and trade stories.

WHEN PLAYING by herself, young Michelle liked traditional girl toys. She baked pretend cakes in her Easy-Bake Oven. She played house with her African American Barbie, complete with its boyfriend, toy house, and car.

Michelle's close-knit family gave her the solid foundation to let her believe she could be anything she wanted to be. But Michelle learned at a young age that not everyone led the life she did. South Shore was surrounded by poor communities. Early on, her heart went out to those who were less fortunate, kids she met in the streets and playground.

School Days

Michelle's parents stressed the importance of getting an education. Both Marian and Frasier skipped a grade in elementary school and later attended college. But neither completed a degree program, something they regretted. Frasier worked full-time to send his four younger siblings to college. Marian never wanted to be the teacher her family thought she should be. She left school to work as a secretary. But Michelle's parents pushed their children to excel in school. "My mother would say, 'When you acquire knowledge, you acquire something no one could take away from you,'" Craig said.

Michelle's parents emphasized reading above any other activities. Both children read books by the age of four, although Michelle took a few months longer to learn than her brother did. Marian brought reading and math workbooks home from school so her children could work ahead. She limited the amount of television Michelle and Craig watched to one hour each day. Homework came first. Michelle and Craig understood that education ranked tops with their parents and always did their best. In the family tradition, both kids skipped second grade.

Teachers found Michelle to be an outstanding student and a class leader. In sixth grade, they chose her for a new class of gifted children. Unlike most of the two thousand students at Bryn Mawr Elementary School, Michelle and her classmates learned Spanish and geometry. They went with teacher Frank Martinez to Kennedy-King College once a week to use the biology lab. Michelle's mother helped chaperone the trips and volunteered in class regularly.

Michelle never minded having her mother along. And she never minded that she towered over her classmates. Michelle walked tall and proud—the way she'd carry herself throughout her life. "Nothing bothered Michelle," Martinez said. "Her height never bothered her. She was always first to volunteer, and she was a straight A student. She always picked her words carefully when talking to you. You could tell by her vocabulary and by talking with her, she would do well."

Michelle continued to excel in seventh- and eighth-grade gifted classes. Her teacher, Solomon Bennett, challenged students with French and algebra. When subjects or activities didn't come naturally, as they did for Craig, Michelle worked harder. She applied the same resolve to everything she tried, including the piano lessons she received from her great-aunt. "She would practice piano for so long you'd have to tell her to stop." Marian said.

Besides reading, writing, and piano, Marian encouraged Michelle and Craig to think, ask questions, and speak their minds. "We told them, 'Make sure you respect your teachers, but don't hesitate to question them. Don't even allow us to just say anything to you. Ask us why.'" As a result, Michelle learned to be honest, respectful of other views, yet willing to speak her mind.

But sometimes Michelle let her temper show. One teacher complained to Marian about Michelle's hot side. Marian's response gave a clue about where Michelle learned her biting sense of humor. Marian said, "Yeah, she's got a temper. But we decided to keep her anyway."

Michelle *(center, back row)* with Mr. Martinez and her sixth-grade class at Bryn Mawr Elementary School. Michelle graduated second in her eighth-grade class.

Teen Years

Michelle graduated second in her eighth-grade class, as her brother had done two years earlier. Craig went to the private Mount Carmel High School to take advantage of its excellent academic and sports programs. Michelle applied to Whitney Young, one of Chicago's best public high schools.

Whitney Young had opened three years earlier as the city's first magnet high school. Magnet schools draw the brightest students of every race and ethnic group from throughout the city.

"Back then, the school was unusual in that it selected enrollment based on test scores," said former classmate Norm Collins. "It was one of the most diverse schools in the city. The 416 students in our class made one big melting pot, and we all got along."

Going to Whitney Young required Michelle to take some risks. She left the comfort of her all-black neighborhood. Instead of a short walk to the local high school, Michelle took hour-long bus and train rides each day. But she thrived at Whitney Young. From the beginning, Michelle's intelligence and focus stood out. She made honor roll each year and was elected to the National Honor Society during her senior year. As a senior, she took advanced placement (AP) classes that counted for college credit.

"I remember Michelle's precision." said Melanie Wojtulewicz, her AP biology teacher. "Her public persona is immaculate. That's how her work was. She was also into literature and very well read. She always carried a book and read outside classes."

"I REMEMBER HER MOST because she made unusual connections between science and humanities. Her favorite teacher was the French teacher, and she knew a lot about French science."
—Melanie Wojtulewicz, Michelle's biology teacher

Michelle, shown here in her senior yearbook photo, was involved in many activities in high school, including student council and the National Honor Society.

Friends recall Michelle as one of the smarter kids. But she also impressed them with her grounded, outgoing personality. "Michelle did everything." Collins said. "She came to parties and football games. She was popular, which helped her become class treasurer. She was trendy, one of the preppy kids stylewise who wore Levi jeans maybe with topside deck shoes or penny loafers."

Michelle liked sports and played baseball, football, soccer, and basketball with her family. But she never played team sports in high school. She didn't want to be typecast because of her height. But her brother saw another reason Michelle never followed him into basketball. "My sister is a poor sport—she didn't like to lose," her brother recalled. "That's why she's been so successful."

Off to College

Michelle possessed a strong sense of fairness. Sometimes that brought out a tough, stubborn streak in her. The ability to persist against tough odds allowed Michelle to attain high goals. For example, she wanted to go to Princeton University, where Craig went. But Michelle's advisers said her test scores weren't high enough for Princeton. "He was getting in everywhere," Michelle recalled. "But I *knew* him and I was like, 'I can do that, too.'" Despite her adviser's warning, she applied to Princeton and was accepted.

Michelle arrived on Princeton's campus in 1981. She was one of ninety-four African Americans in a class

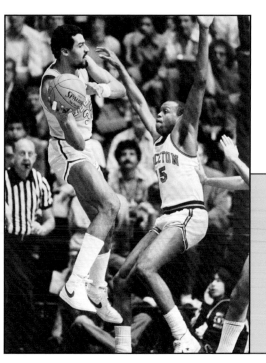

of 1,141 first-year students. For the first time, she ventured far from her Chicago roots. Michelle had flowered in Whitney Young's mixed-race student body, but Princeton felt different.

Michelle's brother Craig *(right)* guards an opponent during a basketball game in 1983. Craig played for the Princeton Tigers and eventually became the school's fourth-highest scorer.

Everyone was from even more academically challenging schools than Michelle. At this wealthy, overwhelmingly white school, she became aware of being black.

"This was the first generation of black students in larger numbers," said Mitchell Duneier, a Princeton professor of sociology (the study of society and social relationships). "Numbers were large enough to hang out with each other on campus and feel the alienation."

The mother of Michelle's roommate disliked her daughter rooming with someone who was black. The mother arranged a room change for her daughter. As Michelle's black classmate Hilary Beard said of the school, "It was a great place to be from. But it was not always a great place to be if you were a minority student."

Michelle majored in sociology with an emphasis on African American studies. As part of a work-study project, Michelle coordinated a tutoring program for local children from poor families. To keep top grades, she studied before breakfast. And she followed a tight schedule throughout her busy day. She earned a reputation as someone who was organized and knew how to get things done.

Outside work and class, however, Michelle struggled with the question of where she belonged at Princeton. Should she hang out with black students or try to mix with whites? Ultimately, Michelle leaned toward black groups and other students of color.

Michelle's struggle with racial identity led her to write a senior thesis titled "Princeton-Educated Blacks and the Black Community." For this paper, she surveyed four hundred African American Princeton alumni. She asked alumni about their experiences at Princeton and their lives since college. She assumed responses would show that successful African Americans had cut themselves off from their black roots. But the survey proved the reverse. They had maintained their ties to the black community, and her final paper reflected these results.

"I believe you can tell a lot about the quality of the mind and kind of person someone is from their thesis," Professor Duneier said. "I do believe she is open-minded and interested in social causes. Whatever she does will be based on evidence and not preconceived ideas."

Becoming a Lawyer

Michelle's thesis results gave her hope. She had promised her father she would use her education and training to give back to their South Side community. Michelle decided the best way to meet the goal of improving the community was to attain an excellent legal education. Graduating from Princeton with honors allowed her to apply to Harvard Law School, another elite school.

Many difficult changes were taking place in the country and on Harvard's campus in 1985. Women and minorities were still struggling to find their rightful place and an equal standing with white men. "Michelle was not intimidated about coming to Harvard and being an advocate

Michelle attended Harvard Law School after graduating from Princeton.

for the downtrodden," said Professor Charles Ogletree, her teacher and adviser at the Black Legal Students Association.

Harvard turned out to be a good fit for Michelle. In class, she had discussions with classmates who came from sheltered, wealthy backgrounds. Michelle challenged them to consider the lives of everyday, poor people who needed lawyers. "She was very probing, very confident. Other students responded very positively to her and her arguments. They would say 'I never thought about that,'" Ogletree said.

Besides attending to classwork, Michelle recruited black students to Harvard and mentored local high school students. She became one of a few volunteers who provided free legal services through the Legal Aid Bureau. The bureau's licensed lawyers supervised students like Michelle as they represented poor families dealing with various issues, such as public housing.

"She would charm and impress people by just walking into the courtroom," Ogletree said. "The way she presented herself and her intelligence were just so noticeable that even judges would look at Michelle to capture every word she'd say.... I was convinced she would become the first African American senator. She had the intelligence, wit, and charm to be a public official."

Earning a Living

Michelle graduated and passed the bar exam to become a lawyer in 1988. Although she dreamed of public service, she had school loans to repay. Community work provided much lower salaries than did the high-powered law firms that offered her jobs. She took an entry-level legal position as associate with Sidley Austin, a top law firm, and moved home with her parents.

Michelle specialized in cases involving one company buying out another and protecting the name and identity of products. Her work impressed clients and coworkers. She quickly earned a reputation for being self-confident, organized, and willing to admit that she still had much to learn. But she never let her low-level position at the firm keep her from speaking out. She pressed for more challenging assignments. She protested actions and rules she thought wrong or unfair. One partner in the firm called her "quite possibly the most ambitious associate that I've ever seen."

Meeting the "Guy with the Funny Name"

During the summer of 1989, the firm assigned Michelle to supervise a summer associate named Barack Obama. Barack had completed his first year at Harvard Law School after working several years as a community organizer on the South Side of Chicago. The office buzzed with how smart and good-looking he was. Michelle, always cautious and down-to-earth, thought that "he sounded too good to be true." Besides, he had a funny name.

Barack immediately fell for his supervisor. But Michelle kept her distance. Men were not in her career plans. Besides, she thought dating a coworker seemed "tacky." She tried to fix him up with friends. Instead, he offered to quit the job so

Michelle met Barack, shown here as a student at Harvard Law School, when he was an intern for the law firm where she worked.

they could date. After several weeks and a basketball game with Craig, Barack finally wore Michelle down. On their first date, they toured Chicago's Art Institute, ate at a restaurant overlooking the city, and saw the Spike Lee movie *Do the Right Thing.* The date swept Michelle off her feet.

But what really impressed Michelle was seeing Barack lead a community meeting soon after their date. She liked that this man devoted his life to helping people in poor communities, particularly those close to hers. He wanted to make a difference. He told the audience never to settle for what is but rather strive for the best. "That is the thread that connects our hearts," Michelle said later.

The two dated after Barack had returned to Harvard and finished law school. Michelle's mother worried that Barack's multicultural heritage would clash with Michelle's midwestern upbringing. His mother was a white woman from Kansas and Hawaii, and his father was a black man from Kenya. Barack had grown up in Hawaii and Indonesia. Craig worried that Barack could never live up to his sister's tough standards.

Time for Change

Michelle longed to do more meaningful work, but she stayed at the law firm. Michelle and Barack became engaged in 1991. Later that year, two events shocked Michelle into considering a change. At the age of fifty-six, her father died suddenly of complications after surgery. And her friend and former Princeton roommate, Suzanne Alele, died of cancer at the age of twenty-five. These sad events prompted Michelle to reevaluate what was important to her. The losses "made me realize I could die tomorrow," she told a reporter. "I had to ask myself, 'Is this how I want to spend my time?' I knew I would never feel a sense of passion or joy about the law."

Michelle's personal life carried her through the sadness. She and Barack continued with wedding plans for the following summer. But she wondered how she could make a difference as Barack had. Besides his previous job as community organizer, he had recently published his autobiography, *Dreams from My Father*, and was practicing law at a firm that served poor communities.

Michelle discussed her plans for public service with a friend who connected her with Valerie Jarrett, then deputy chief of staff for Chicago mayor Richard M. Daley. Jarrett offered Michelle a job at their first meeting. Before accepting, Michelle asked Jarrett to meet her fiancé. Barack wanted to make sure the job would prepare Michelle for the community work she sought. Jarrett and her job passed Barack's test.

Michelle followed Jarrett to another city job, commissioner of planning and development. Their job was to promote and expand city business. Those who worked with Michelle described her as direct—a problem solver and a good manager.

Wedding Bells

Before they married, Barack took Michelle to meet his families. They traveled to rural Kenya, where Barack's step-siblings and step-grandmother lived. They made the first of their annual Christmas visits to Honolulu, where Barack's grandparents, mother, and stepsister lived. Michelle charmed people wherever she went.

The wedding took place on October 3, 1992, at Trinity United Church of Christ. The wedding party looked like the United Nations. Guests came from Kenya, Indonesia,

Family helped Michelle celebrate her wedding to Barack, including Barack's sister Maya *(far left)*, Michelle's mother Marian *(second from left)*, and Barack's sister Auma *(second from right)*.

and Hawaii and represented every stage of both Barack and Michelle's lives.

"When I heard they had gotten together, I remember saying to myself, 'that's perfect,'" said David Wilkins, a Harvard Law School professor who knew them both. "She's the grounded and supportive person he needs to do things he wanted to do. And he, in turn, would respect what she could do."

Encouraging Young People

After eighteen months with the city, Michelle seized an opportunity to work directly with promising young people. In 1993 she launched the Chicago branch of Public Allies, an AmeriCorps program that trains and encourages young people through work at government and community organizations. As director, Michelle recruited and organized volunteers who committed a year to provide public service in low-income areas. She trained them to pinpoint and build on the positive traits of people in these neighborhoods. This approach ran counter to most helping organizations that saw poor people as problems rather than resources. After three years, Michelle had raised enough money to secure Public Allies' future, and she had built a solid organization.

"One of the things I came to appreciate about her was how comfortably she moved in different situations, from connecting with the eighteen-year-old gangbanger to single moms from housing projects to executives to fund-raisers," said Jody Kretzmann, a Northwestern University professor who worked with Michelle on training.

Michelle's passion for community work, leadership skills, and city hall connections made her well known around Chicago. Over the years, she was asked to join boards running six different community and business organizations.

Meanwhile, Barack decided to run for Illinois state senator. Although she knew he wanted a life in politics, Michelle thought this was a pipe dream. She was sure he was a better person than some of the self-serving politicians she had seen. She thought he could make more meaningful changes in the community through his work at the law firm. "It seems like a dirty business, and Barack is such a nice guy," she told a reporter. "I thought, eventually he'll come to his senses." But he didn't.

In 1996 South Side Chicagoans elected Barack Obama to office. Voters came from the Hyde Park neighborhood, where the couple lived. This middle-income, mixed-race neighborhood included the University of Chicago, where Barack taught at the law school. In surrounding areas, however, residents struggled with poverty, poor housing, and ineffective schools.

As Barack settled into the state senate, the university hired Michelle to start a volunteer program similar to Public Allies. The university wanted to be a better neighbor to the surrounding poor areas. For four years, she created, then expanded opportunities for university students and staff to interact with residents from nearby neighborhoods. By the time Michelle took a new job at the University of Chicago Medical School, the university program she had begun was placing more than two thousand student volunteers a year in about 150 local organizations.

Juggling Work and Family

During this time, Michelle and Barack wanted to expand their family. Malia was born on July 4, 1998, and Natasha, called Sasha, arrived three years later. Because Barack pursued higher government office that kept him from home, most family chores fell to Michelle.

Tension developed between Barack and Michelle. She had hoped to raise their children as she was raised,

Barack, with Michelle and Malia, gives a speech after losing the primary election for U.S. House of Representatives in 2000.

with cozy evenings where everyone ate dinner together. But as state senator, Barack often stayed in Springfield. Campaigning for reelection took even more time away from the family. After many arguments, Michelle ultimately supported Barack's decision to stay in politics.

In January 2003, Barack announced his run for the U.S. Senate. By then Michelle had been promoted to vice president of community relations at the hospital. Her two-person office staff had expanded to seventeen, and the number of employees volunteering outside the hospital had reached eight hundred.

Barack won the 2004 Senate election. He and Michelle decided she and the kids would stay in Chicago, while he

The Obama family in 2004, when Barack won election to the U.S. Senate, *(left to right)* Malia, Barack, Michelle, and Sasha

worked in Washington, D.C. Longtime family and friends supported Michelle in her juggling act as a working mom. "I'm pretty private and like to surround myself with people that I trust and love," she once said.

On the Campaign Trail

After a little more than a year as U.S. senator, Barack considered running for president. Michelle worried about what a run for president would mean for their family. They were set moneywise. Barack's second book, *The Audacity of Hope*, had been a huge success, so they were free of debt for the first time. Book sales paid off college debts and let them buy a larger home.

Still, Michelle wanted assurance he could win. Barack's managers pointed to the hundreds of people nationwide who attended his book signings, a good indication of his popularity. Eventually, Michelle agreed that the time was right for Barack to run. On Saturday, February 10, 2007, in Springfield, Illinois, Barack announced he would run for president of the United States. Applauding him on that freezing day were Michelle, Malia, and Sasha.

Michelle still disliked politics. But she disliked losing even more. She threw herself into the campaign. She saw Barack's candidacy as a real opportunity to change the nation's direction. Michelle knew what he could do and wanted to let others know too.

To become more involved in the campaign, Michelle took a leave of absence from her job at the hospital. She asked Marian to care for Malia and Sasha. Michelle wanted the children's schedule kept constant while she traveled from state to state. Michelle even arranged her travel so she could return home each night to help the girls with homework and tuck them into bed.

Many campaign advisers saw Michelle's involvement as a boost to her husband's campaign. Michelle's experiences juggling work and family spoke to women struggling with similar issues. As a black woman who grew up in an African American neighborhood, African Americans could relate to her story and to Barack's. She told stories—about Barack taking out the garbage and leaving the butter out after breakfast—that made him seem more human. She also emphasized how he wanted people to hope for a better world rather than settle for what is.

Opponents seized every chance to discredit Michelle and her growing popularity. When she mentioned that her husband's success with potential voters made her "proud of her country for the first time," critics spoke out against her. They combed through her past and even read old copies of her thesis to find information. They picked at everything from her arched eyebrows to the fist bump she gave Barack. They used these details to misrepresent her as an angry black woman.

Campaign managers moved to tamp down criticism. They arranged for a media tour to let voters see for themselves how warm and capable Michelle was. Michelle appeared on major television talk shows. With each appearance, she charmed audiences with her down-to-earth sense of humor. She showed people why Barack calls her his supportive "rock."

People also began to notice Michelle's style. It seemed to match her no-nonsense, practical image. Tall, thin, and smartly dressed, Michelle made an instant impact on fashion. Designers liked her simple, colorful look. Many women bought the affordable styles that she wore. Michelle appeared on a number of national best-dressed lists.

Inauguration Day

On November 4, 2008, Barack was elected president of the United States, and the Obama family life changed forever. Michelle began a whirlwind of activities. But her first priority was her daughters' well-being. She chose a school for Malia and Sasha. To help keep her daughters grounded, Michelle asked her mother to come live with them in the White House. Marian, also a private person, reluctantly agreed.

On Inauguration Day, January 20, 2009, almost two million people stood, some for more than six hours, to witness Barack Obama being sworn in as president. As her husband took the oath of office, Michelle held the Bible, the same one that Abraham Lincoln had used in 1861 when he became president. After the swearing in, she and Barack walked part of the parade route down Pennsylvania Avenue. That night they danced at ten balls. Then they went to their new home, the White House. On this day, Michelle had become First Lady and the Obamas had become the first African American family to occupy the White House. The Obamas shined as role models. Black children could now

Barack and Michelle walk along Pennsylvania Avenue during the Inauguration Parade on January 20, 2009.

Michelle points to a student during a visit to a public school in Washington, D.C., in February 2009. She plans to focus on education and family issues during her time as First Lady.

dream of one day becoming president.

After the inauguration, the real work began. Michelle helped her daughters settle into school as ninety-three staff members helped her organize the White House for dinners, performances, and other events. At the same time, Michelle focused on making a difference as First Lady. She pushed to ease the burdens of working women and military families. She visited schools and championed education improvements. Whatever she did, she promised to ensure that her role as First Lady benefited everyday individuals and families.

"She's not at all about being famous or rich," said David Wilkins, one of her law school professors. "She was going to do important work and have an important impact on people around her." She has done that and more, but the best is yet to come.

IMPORTANT DATES

1964   Michelle is born on January 17 in Chicago, Illinois.

1977   She graduates from Bryn Mawr Elementary School.

1981   She graduates from Whitney Young High School.

1985   Michelle earns her degree in sociology from Princeton University.

1988   She graduates from Harvard Law School. She joins the law firm of Sidley Austin.

1989   She meets Barack Obama.

1990   She works as deputy chief of staff with the city of Chicago.

1991   Frasier Robinson III, Michelle's father, dies.

1992   She moves into an assistant commissioner job for Chicago's Department of Planning and Development.

She marries Barack Obama on October 3.

1993 She becomes founder and executive director of the Chicago Public Allies.

1996 Michelle joins the University of Chicago as associate dean of student services.
Barack wins election as Illinois state senator.

1997 Michelle launches the University of Chicago Community Service Center.

1998 Malia is born.

2001 Natasha, known as Sasha, is born.

2002 Michelle becomes vice president of community and external affairs at the University of Chicago Medical Center.

2004 Barack is elected U.S. senator from Illinois.

2007–2008 Michelle campaigns for her husband's run for U.S. president.

2008 Barack is elected the forty-fourth president of the United States and the first African American to hold the office.

2009 Michelle becomes the nation's first African American First Lady.

GLOSSARY

alienation: separation or withdrawal of a person

alumni: graduates of a given school, college, or university

chaperone: a person who accompanies young people at school or social gatherings

Democrat: a member or supporter of the Democratic Party

discrimination: prejudicial outlook, action, or treatment

filtration plant: a place where germs are filtered, or removed, from the water supply

fund-raisers: people or events that raise money for charities, political parties, candidates, or other causes

hostility: deep-seated ill will

lectern: a stand used for a speaker's notes

multiple sclerosis: a disease that causes nerve damage and difficulty in muscle control

segregated: set apart, or separated

sociology: the study of society and social relationships

unions: organized groups of workers

SOURCE NOTES

8 Susan A. Jones, ed., *Michelle Obama: In Her Own Words* (Scotts Valley, CA: CreateSpace, 2008), 39.

9 Ibid., 35.

11 Stephen Garnett, author interview, December 16, 2008.

13 Shailagh Murray, "A Family Tree Rooted in American Soil," *Washington Post*, October 1, 2008, http://www .washingtonpost.com/wpdyn/ content/story/2008/10/10/ ST2008100103245.html (November 27, 2008).

15 Melinda Henneberger, "Michelle Obama Interview: Her Father's Daughter," *Reader's Digest*, October 2008, http://www .rd.com/your-america-inspiring -people-and-stories/michelle -obama-interview-her-fathers -daughter/article98945.html (November 27, 2008).

15 Ibid.

17 Michael Powell and Jodi Kantor, "After Attacks, Michelle Obama Looks for a New Introduction," *New York Times*, June 18, 2009, A1.

18 Jodi Kantor, "A Portrait of Change: The Nation's Many Faces in Extended First Family," *New York Times*, January 21, 2009, A1.

18 Frank Martinez, author interview, January 20, 2009.

18 Karen Springen, "First Lady in Waiting," *Chicago Magazine*, October 2004, http://www .chicagomagazine.com/ chicago-Magazine/October- 2004/First-Lady-in-Waiting (November 27, 2008).

18 Elizabeth Lightfoot, *Michelle Obama: First Lady of Hope* (Guilford, CT: Lyons Press 2009), 5.

20 Ibid., 6.

20 Norm Collins, author interview, December 14, 2008.

20 Ibid.

21 Melanie Wojtulewicz, author interview, January 16, 2009.

21 Collins.

22 Holly Yeager, "The Heart and Mind of Michelle Obama," *'O' Magazine*, 2004, http://www .oprah.com/article/omagazine/ ss_omag_200711_mobama (January 30, 2009).

23 Richard Wolffe, "Barack's Rock," Newsweek, February 25, 2008, http://www.newsweek .com/id/112849 (March 18, 2009).

23 Mitchell Duneier, author interview, December 15, 2008.

24 Ibid.

24–25 Ibid.

25 Charles Ogletree, author interview, January 23, 2009.

26 Ibid.

26 Ibid.

27 Liza Mundy, *Michelle: A Biography* (New York: Simon & Schuster, 2008), 91.

27 David Mendel, *Obama: From Promise to Power* (New York: HarperCollins, 2007), 93.

28 Stacy St. Clair, "Scenes from Obamas' Love Story," *Chicago Tribune*, November 30, 2008, Section 1, 4.

29 Ibid.

31 Lightfoot, 33.

31–32 David Wilkins, author interview, February 2, 2009.

32 Jody Kretzmann, author interview, November 12, 2008.

35 Henneberger, 1.

39 Mariana Cook, "A Couple in Chicago," *New Yorker*, January 19, 2009, http://www.newyorker.com/reporting/2009/01/19/090119fa_fact_cookon (January 21, 2009).

SELECTED BIBLIOGRAPHY

The author drew from more than one hundred newspaper and magazine articles nationwide, several reputable websites, countless television and Web interviews, as well as her own personal interviews in writing this biography. The following offers a sampling of these resources:

Cook, Mariana. "A Couple in Chicago." *New Yorker*, January 19, 2009. http://www.newyorker.com/reporting/2009/01/19/090119fa_fact_cookon (January 19, 2009)

Felsenthal, Carol. "Michelle: A Chicago Story," *Chicago Magazine*, February 2009, 50–59.

Gittley, Kalari. "Discovering Hyde Park." *Hyde Park Herald*, February 14, 2007, 5–18.

Henneberger, Melinda. "Michelle Obama Interview: Her Father's Daughter." *Reader's Digest*, October 2008, http://www.rd.com/ your-america-inspiring-people-and-stories/michelle-obama-interview-her-fathers-daughter/article98945.html (March 18, 2009).

Jones, Susan A., ed. *Michelle Obama: In Her Own Words*. Scotts Valley, CA: CreateSpace, 2008.

Kantor, Jodi. "A Portrait of Change: The Nation's Many Faces in Extended First Family." *New York Times*, January 21, 2009, A1.

Lightfoot, Elizabeth. *Michelle Obama: First Lady of Hope*. Guilford, CT: Lyons Press, 2009.

Mundy, Liza. *Michelle: A Biography*. New York: Simon & Schuster, 2008.

Murray, Shailagh. "A Family Tree Rooted in American Soil." *Washington Post*, October 1, 2008. http://www .washingtonpost.com/wpdyn/content/story/2008/10/10/ ST2008100103245.html (November 27, 2008).

Obama, Barack. *The Audacity of Hope*. New York: Crown, 2006.

——. *Dreams from My Father*. New York: Three Rivers Press, 2004.

Rossi, Rosalind. "The Woman Behind Obama." *Chicago Sun-Times*, January 20, 2007. http://www.suntimes.com/news/ politics/obama/221458,CST-NWS-mich21.article (March 18, 2009)

Springen, Karen. "First Lady in Waiting." *Chicago Magazine*, October, 2004. http://www.chicagomagazine.com/chicago-Magazine/October-2004/First-Lady-in-Waiting (November 27, 2008).

Wolffe, Richard. "Barack's Rock." *Newsweek*, February 25, 2008, http://www.newsweek.com/id/112849 (March 18, 2009).

Yeager, Holly. "The Heart and Mind of Michelle Obama." *'O' Magazine*, 2004. http://www.oprah.com/article/omagazine/ss_omag_200711_mobama (January 30, 2009).

FURTHER READING

Brill, Marlene Targ. *Barack Obama: President for a New Era.* Minneapolis: Lerner Publishing Company, 2009.

Brophy, David. *Michelle Obama: Meet the First Lady.* New York: Collins, 2009

Colbert, David. *Michelle Obama: An American Story.* New York: Houghton Mifflin, 2009.

"First Lady Michelle Obama"
http://www.whitehouse.gov/adminstration/michelle_obama
The White House posts a biography and other current information about the First Lady.

"Michelle Obama Speech at the Democratic National Convention"
http://www.elections.nytimes.com/2008/president/conventions/videos/20080825_OBAMA_SPEECH
This site reproduces the speech Michelle Obama made at the 2008 Democratic convention.

INDEX

Page numbers in *italics* refer to illustrations.

ACKNOWLEDGMENTS

Neither Michelle Obama nor Barack Obama has agreed to cooperate with authors of their biographies. That means authors must play detective to find kind souls who agree to provide leads and interviews. I want to thank Yvonne Bennett, Norm Collins, Mitchell Duneier, Stephen Garnett, Jody Kretzmann, Frank Martinez, Professor Charles Ogletree, Melanie Wojtulewicz, and Professor David Wilkins for sharing their insights about Michelle Obama. And I am indebted to the following people who helped me track down these people and additional information: Bob Bures, Retired Teachers Association of Chicago; John McNight at Northwestern University; Dr. Robert Magrisso; Frances Radencil at the Chicago Teacher's Union Pension Board; Cathy Lynn Reed, Historical Chicago Bungalow Initiative; and Beth Takekawa, Wing Luke Asian Museum. A hearty thank-you to all of you who helped me with this book.